入门篇
Beginning Level

汉语十日通
Chinese in 10 Days

程璐璐 主编

Reading & Writing

顾　　问　翟　艳

主　　编　程璐璐

副 主 编　刘　硕

编　　者　黄雯雯　翟　甜　龙　波

英文翻译　高　娜

＃ 前　言

　　《汉语十日通·读写》是在"三位一体"教学模式下为零起点汉语学习者编写的一套读写技能教材。"三位一体"教学模式，即读写课与听说课基于综合课教学内容拓展技能训练，以便在夯实综合语言能力的基础上，更好地突出技能训练的特点。《汉语十日通·读写》在综合教材《汉语十日通》所教授的语言知识、话题及文化内容的基础上，有扩展，有提升，帮助学习者在充分的练习中提高读写技能。

　　编写本套教材的指导思想是：突出读和写的语言技能操练，主要集中于对汉字文本的阅读与理解、汉字的认读与书写、汉语遣词造句与写作等读写技能进行强化训练。综合课的语言要素学习为技能训练提供了主题、基本词汇和语法的基本用法。本书在技能操练方面进行强化，并适当扩展了话题的范围，补充了适当的词语，使语法意义在更广阔的环境中得到应用。教学的原则是：尊重认知和习得的规律，先输入再输出，先阅读后写作，大量输入，适度输出；汉字先认读后书写，先建立形音义联系，再进行书写练习。

　　全书共四册，分为入门篇、基础篇、提高篇、冲刺篇。每册10课，完成一课的全部教学内容需要2课时，全四册共需80课时。教师也可根据本单位教学计划和教学目标等教学实际情况灵活选用教材内容，并适当增减读写课时。

　　四册教材在编写体例上大体相同，又根据学生语言水平的变化，在细节上有所调整。以入门篇为例，主要包括以下模块：

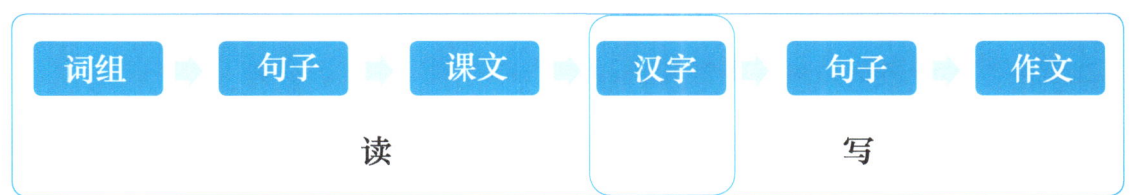

　　读词组　　提供更丰富的词语组合，通过认读，帮助学生在不同组合关系中熟悉生词，适应汉字文本认读与理解，同时，在组合关系中潜移默化地培养语法感。

读句子 该模块强调有意义的认读。在汉字文本认读的基础上，巩固记忆，加深理解。以句子为单位的语义理解，可以为篇章理解训练做好准备。

读课文 课文的编写充分调用学生应知应会的词汇、语法要素，为学习者提供多样的可懂性阅读输入材料。课文配有多种形式的练习，帮助学生理解文义。入门阶段开始便渗透阅读策略，培养良好的阅读习惯。如从第1课到第9课，每一课都设置了推测词义的题型，学生可以根据字形、语素、语法关系、上下文等语言知识和阅读策略进行猜测。这些词语，以补充词表的形式，附于教材正文后。

读写汉字 包括"学一学"和"练一练"两个部分。"学一学"包含学习本课生字、介绍汉字基础知识。生字的排序依据综合课生词表的顺序。"练一练"设计了多种练习形式，包括认字、形音义练习、书写汉字等。

写句子 在熟练掌握汉字书写与字词意义的基础上，进行以句子为单位的写作练习。从完成句子逐步过渡到看图并用词造句，对标HSK四级考试的书写测试要求。

第10课为复习课，目的是在前九课学习的基础上，进行归纳、整理和提升。如复习本册书的主要表达方式、完成篇章写作等。

这套教材汇集了汉语阅读教学与研究的成果和一线教师的教学实践经验，具有以下特点：

1. 读写与综合既互相支撑，又分工明确。

《汉语十日通·读写》依托《汉语十日通》的语言要素进行阅读技能训练，能够提高综合课语言要素掌握的熟巧程度，有利于将语言知识转换成语言能力；同时，《读写》并没有止步于支撑综合课，而是在此基础上，对各项读写微技能提出了更高的训练要求，以满足对读写要求高的学习者的学习需求。

2. 难度循序渐进，兼具可懂性和挑战性。

"读"从词组、句子过渡到篇章，"写"从字到句再到篇，内容安排由易到难，层层递进。课文是核心部分。课文的编写，依据学生当前掌握的语言知识，保证输入的可懂性；同时，提供语言丰富多样的表达，设计精巧的"阅读障碍"，让学生在挑战中，学习阅读策略，提升阅读技能。

前言

3. 以阅读带动识字，帮助学生快速适应汉字文本。

我们借鉴了汉语母语儿童在阅读中习得汉字的经验，以及英语分级阅读的教育理念，将"汉字"模块安排在词组、句子、课文（篇章阅读）模块之后。学习者在阅读中充分理解意义并建立形音义联系之后，认读和书写汉字，效率更高，效果更好。

4. 对标新大纲，考教结合，以考促学。

补充词表的词条和生字表中的汉字，均根据《国际中文教育中文水平等级标准》标注了等级，方便教师和学习者了解。1～6分别对应一至六级；7表示高等，对应七到九级；＊表示超纲。部分练习采用了与HSK3～4级相同或相似的题型，便于有考级需求的学习者提前熟悉考试。

5. 读写教材与综合教材、习字本等灵活组合，满足不同需求。

《汉语十日通·读写》与《汉语十日通》《汉语十日通·听说》为"三位一体"系列教材，是互相支撑、互相促动的关系。此外，十日通系列教材还配有综合课练习册和习字本。教师或教学单位，可根据教学目标和教学需求，灵活组合。

本教材已经过三年的试用和打磨，是团队集体智慧的结晶。希望这样一套读写教材，能够让汉语汉字读写不再难学。

Preface

Chinese in 10 Days · Reading & Writing is a series of reading and writing Chinese textbooks developed for beginning learners of Chinese as second language under the "Three in One" teaching mode. The "Three in One" teaching mode refers to skill training with respect to reading and writing, as well as listening and speaking based on the contents of the comprehensive course. It highlights the training of skills on the basis of enhanced comprehensive language competence.

Specifically, not only was the *Chinese in 10 Days · Reading & Writing* derived from the language knowledge, topics and cultural contents introduced in the comprehensive textbooks of *Chinese in 10 Days*, it also includes expanded and extended contents and activities to help learners improve their reading and writing skills through sufficient practice.

The guiding philosophy of compiling this series of teaching materials is to highlight the language skill training in reading and writing, mainly focusing on the intensive training of reading and writing skills, such as comprehending Chinese texts, recognizing and writing Chinese characters, making sentences or writing paragraphs in Chinese. The learning of linguistic elements in the comprehensive course provides topics, basic vocabulary and the basic usage of grammar for skill training. The current series of textbooks are to enhance skill training, in terms of appropriately expanding the scope of topics, providing more words, and applying the grammatical meanings in a broader context.

The teaching approaches include: respecting the rules of cognition and acquisition, inputting before outputting, reading before writing, and moderate output based on sufficient input; as for the Chinese characters, recognizing goes before writing, and the relationship among their form, sound, and meaning is to be established, followed with writing practice.

Preface

The whole series consists of four volumes: the beginning level, the elementary level, the intermediate level and the advanced level. Each volume includes 10 lessons and each lesson takes 2 class-hours to complete, totaling at 80 class-hours for the entire 4 volumes. Teachers may also decide what to teach from the textbooks, and/or adjust the length of class hours based on specific needs.

The compilation of the four volumes basically follows the same principles, while detailed adjustments have also been made in accordance with students' language development. Taking the beginning volume as an example, it mainly includes the following sections:

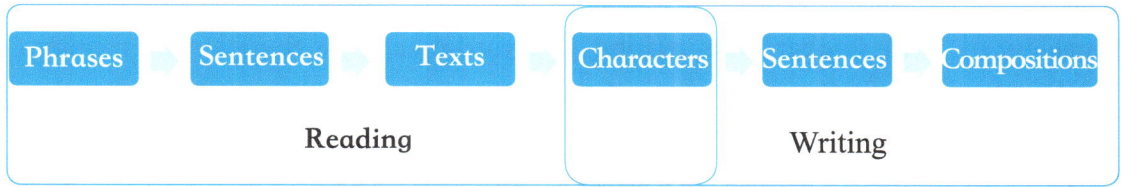

Reading phrases　　Plentiful phrases are provided in this section to help students get familiar with new words in various combinations, and get used to reading and comprehending Chinese texts. Meanwhile, students' sense of grammar is also expected to be improved in the process.

Reading sentences　　This section emphasizes meaningful reading. Based on recognizing and reading Chinese characters, the current section helps students with memory and understanding of Chinese. Intensive sentence comprehension practice can get students well prepared for understanding paragraphs and passages.

Reading texts　　The compilation of the texts intends to utilize students' prior knowledge of vocabulary and grammar, and to provide them with various comprehensible reading materials. Various forms of exercises are designed to help students understand the meaning of the texts. Training for reading strategies is also considered at the beginning level to form good reading habits of students. For example, practice for anticipating word meaning is placed from Lesson 1 to Lesson 9. Students are to be trained to guess word meanings relying on language knowledge and reading strategies, such as glyph, morpheme, grammatical relationship and context. These words are attached to the textbooks as supplementary vocabulary.

Reading and writing characters   This section consists of two parts: "Let's learn" and "Let's practice". "Let's learn" includes learning new words and introducing the basic knowledge of Chinese characters. The characters are listed in the same order as that of the word lists in the comprehensive textbooks of *Chinese in 10 Days*. "Let's practice" offers a variety of exercises in many forms, including character recognition, form-sound-meaning practice, and Chinese characters writing.

Writing sentences   This section is about practicing sentence writing based on the mastery of Chinese characters writing and word meanings. Students are required to complete sentences, or to use given words to make sentences for given pictures. This part corresponds roughly to the HSK 4 standards for writing.

Lesson 10 is a review lesson. The purpose of this lesson is to summarize prior knowledge and improve students' reading and writing skills on the basis of previous nine lessons. For example, this lesson reviews the main expressions in this book and the composition completion tasks.

This series of teaching materials integrates the findings of Chinese reading-and-writing teaching and research with practical teaching experience from front-line teachers. It has the following features:

1. The Reading & Writing Course and the Comprehensive Course are complementary to each other while focusing on different teaching objectives

Chinese in 10 Days · Reading & Writing is based on the linguistic elements of the comprehensive textbooks to carry out reading skills training, which can improve students' proficiency of linguistic elements acquired from the comprehensive course, and it is conducive to converting language knowledge into language competence. At the same time, *Reading & Writing* not only supports the comprehensive course, but also puts forward training requirements for various reading and writing micro-skills to meet learning needs of learners who aim higher in mastering Chinese reading and writing skills.

2. The level of difficulty goes up step by step with both comprehensibility and challenge

"Reading" starts from phrases and sentences to chapters, and "writing" begins from characters to sentences and then to chapters. The exercises are arranged from easy ones to difficult ones. Texts in each lesson form the core part. The texts were compiled according to language knowledge that students have acquired to ensure the comprehensibility of inputs. Meanwhile, rich and diverse language expressions and well-designed reading "obstacles/puzzles" are provided. Students can learn reading strategies and improve their reading skills through these challenging activities.

3. Learning Chinese characters through exposure to reading materials helps students familiarize themselves quickly with Chinese texts

Drawing on the experience how native Chinese-speaking children acquire Chinese characters in reading and the ideas of leveled English reading, the "Characters" section in the current book is placed after the phrase, sentence and text (passage reading) sections. More efficient and effective outcomes are expected if Chinese learners start to recognize and write Chinese characters after their full comprehension of the reading materials with the connection between form, sound and meaning of Chinese characters formed.

4. In line with the latest syllabus, examination and teaching are combined while learning is facilitated through preparations for the exams

For the convenience of teachers and learners, each entry in the Supplementary New Words and the new character list is marked with a grade number according to the *Chinese Proficiency Grading Standards for International Chinese Language Education*. The numbers 1~6 correspond to level 1 to level 6 respectively, and 7 indicates the advanced levels of level 7~9, and * indicates words not included in the syllabus. Part of the exercises adopt the same or similar question types of HSK 3~4, which can help learners get familiar with the exams if needed.

5. The Reading and Writing textbooks can be used together with the comprehensive textbooks and exercise books to meet different needs

Chinese in 10 Days · Reading & Writing, *Chinese in 10 Days* and *Chinese in 10 Days · Listening & Speaking* are the "Three in One" series textbooks, which complement and facilitate each other. In addition, this series of textbooks is completed with student books and exercise books for practicing writing Chinese characters. Teachers or institutes may choose teaching materials from the series according to their specific teaching objectives and needs.

This textbook has been used and revised by front-line teachers for three years, and it is the fruition of collective wisdom. We hope that such a set of reading and writing textbooks will make the reading and writing of Chinese characters no longer a difficult endeavor.

来，认识一下！

Come and get to know the characters!

他们是谁？请试着写一写他们的名字。**Who are they? Please try to write down their names.**

提示：参考《汉语十日通》综合教材入门篇中的"主要人物"。**Tips: You can check the "Main Characters" in *Chinese in 10 Days* (Beginning Level).**

试一试：下面的名字怎么读？ How to read the following names in Chinese? Have a try!

王兰　　　　　丁强　　　　　白丽娜　　　　　马小美

附加任务：猜一猜，这些名字的主人是男的还是女的？去课本里找一找答案吧！ Extra task: Are these names for male or female? Guess and look for the answer in the textbook.

目 录 Contents

第 1 课	1
第 2 课	5
第 3 课	10
第 4 课	15
第 5 课	20
第 6 课	26
第 7 课	32
第 8 课	38
第 9 课	45
第 10 课	51
附　录	58

参考答案

第 1 课

一、词组：认读 Read the phrases

你们　　　学生们　　　老师们　　　你好　　　您好　　　老师好

再见　　　谢谢　　　不客气　　　对不起　　　没关系

谢谢你　　　谢谢你们　　　谢谢您　　　谢谢老师

一三五七九　　　二四六八十

二、句子：认读并连线 Read and match

1. 老师好！　　　A. 不客气！

2. 再见！　　　　B. 你们好！

3. 谢谢！　　　　C. 没关系！

4. 对不起！　　　D. 再见！

三、对话 & 短文：认读并完成练习 Read the dialogue or passage and do the exercises

（一）

A：老师，谢谢您！

B：不客气！

A：老师，再见！

B：再见！

□ 读后填空 Fill in the blanks with proper words

A 是 shì (to be) _____，B 是 _____。

（二）

十！九！八！七！六！五！四！三！二！一！

□ 选一选 Choose the proper picture according to the text

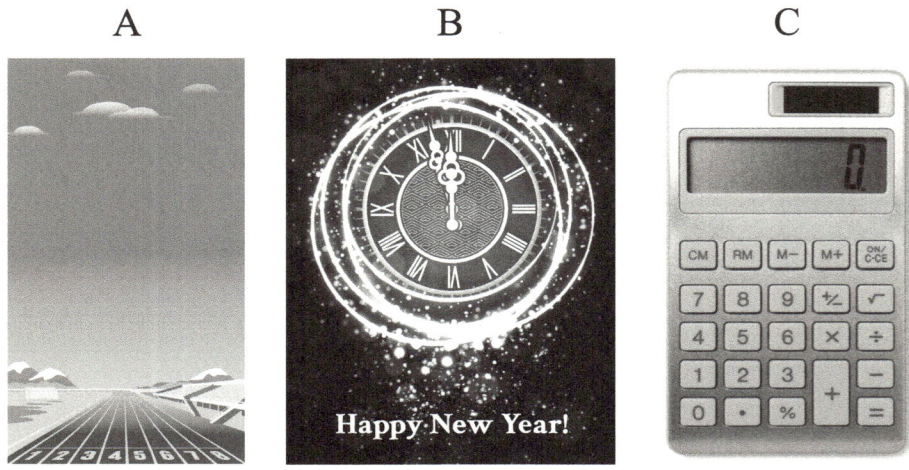

A   B   C

四、汉字 Characters

（一）学一学 Let's learn

你¹ 好¹ 您¹ 们¹ 老¹ 师¹ 谢¹ 不¹ 客¹ 气¹ 对¹ 起¹
没¹ 关¹ 系¹ 一¹ 二¹ 三¹ 四¹ 五¹ 六¹ 七¹ 八¹ 九¹
十¹ 学¹ 生¹ 再¹ 见¹

1. 汉字的基本笔画 Basic strokes of Chinese characters

笔画 Stroke	名称 Name	书写方法 Way to write	例字 Example
、	diǎn 点	↘	六
一	héng 横	→	二
丨	shù 竖	↓	十
丿	piě 撇	↙	八
乀	nà 捺	↘	八
✓	tí 提	↗	没

2. 汉字的基本笔顺① Basic stroke order of Chinese characters ①

规则 Rule	例字 Example	笔顺 Stroke order
xiān héng hòu shù 先 横 后 竖	十	一 十
xiān piě hòu nà 先 撇 后 捺	八	丿 八
xiān zuǒ hòu yòu 先 左 后 右	你	亻 你
xiān shàng hòu xià 先 上 后 下	学	𭁳 学

（二）练一练 Let's practice

1. 给汉字加拼音并把汉字与相应的数字连起来 Mark the characters with *pinyin* and match them with the numbers

1 2 3 4 5 6 7 8 9 10

(　) (　) (　) (　) (　) (　) (　) (　) (yī) (　)

三　五　七　九　八　二　十　四　一　六

2. 写汉字 Write down the words in Chinese characters according to the context and *pinyin*

（1）A：谢谢您！

　　　B：_____。（bú kèqi）

（2）A：对不起！

　　　B：_____。（méi guānxi）

（3）_____！（zàijiàn）

第 2 课

一、词组：认读 Read the phrases

很好　　　　很忙　　　　　很累

不好　　　　不忙　　　　（correct）
　　　　　　　　　　　　不对

好学生　　　好老师　　　好爸爸　　　好妈妈

哥哥姐姐们　　　　　　　弟弟妹妹们

二、句子：认读并连线 Read and match

1. 奶奶，您累吗？　　　　A. 没关系。

2. 姐姐，对不起！　　　　B. 他很忙。

3. 你哥哥忙吗？　　　　　C. 他们很好，谢谢！

4. 你爸爸妈妈好吗？　　　D. 我不累。

三、对话 & 短文：认读并完成练习 Read the dialogue or passage and do the exercises

（一）

A：王老师好！

B：你好！

A：老师，您忙吗？

B：我很忙。

A：老师，您累吗？

B：我不累。谢谢你！

A：不客气。再见！

☐ 读后填空 Fill in the blanks with proper words

王老师不_____，但是他很_____。

dànshì（but）

（二）

你们好！我很好！我很忙，我不累。

我爸爸很忙，我妈妈不忙。

我爷爷很好，我奶奶很好。

老师们很累，学生们很累。

☐ 读后判断对错 True or false（√/×）

（1）我很累。　　　　　　　　　　　　（　）

（2）我爸爸不忙。　　　　　　　　　　（　）

（3）我爷爷奶奶很好。　　　　　　　　（　）

（4）老师们很累，学生们不累。　　　　（　）

四、汉字 Characters

（一）学一学 Let's learn

爸¹ 妈¹ 忙¹ 吗¹ 爷¹ 奶¹ 累¹ 我¹ 他¹ 她¹ 很¹ 哥¹ 弟¹ 姐¹ 妹¹

1. 汉字的派生笔画① Derived strokes of Chinese characters ①

笔画 Stroke	名称 Name	例字 Example
乛	héngzhé 横折	五
𠃌	héngpiě 横撇	好
ㄥ	shùzhé 竖折	忙
㇄	shùtí 竖提	(meal) 饭
ㄴ	shùwān 竖弯	四
ㄥ	piězhé 撇折	系
㇄	piědiǎn 撇点	好

2. 汉字的基本结构① Basic structures of Chinese characters ①

结构 Structure		例字 Example	图解 Illustration
dútǐzì 独体字 Single-component		不	□
hétǐzì 合体字 Multi-component	zuǒ-yòu jiégòu 左右结构 Left-right	你、忙	□□
	shàng-xià jiégòu 上下结构 Top-bottom	爸、您	□/□

第 2 课

3. 偏旁① Radicals ①

偏旁 Radical	名称 Name	例字 Example	说明 Explanation
亻	dānrénpáng 单人旁	你、他	rén（person） 人
女	nǚzìpáng 女字旁	她、好	nǚ（female） 女
心	xīnzìdǐ 心字底	您	xīn（heart） 心
忄	shùxīnpáng 竖心旁	忙	

一个汉字作为偏旁出现时，笔形往往会有一些变化。如，"女"的最后一笔是"一"（héng），但作为女字旁写在左边时，最后一笔是"㇂"（tí）。Most radicals, which indicate meaning, came from normal characters but often write differently. For example, the last stroke of the character 女 is written as 一 (héng), while of the radical 女 as ㇂ (tí).

（二）练一练 Let's practice

1. 圈出每组一样的汉字并写在方格中 Circle the same character in each group and write it in the box

（1）对不起！

不客气！

（2）老师好！

我很好。

（3）您累吗？

谢谢您！

2. 根据结构类型给下列汉字分类 Put the characters into different groups according to the structures

我	累	气	吗
师	学	生	客
爷	对	弟	没

☐ : _____

☐ : _____

☐ : _____

第 2 课

☐ **3. 圈出下列汉字的偏旁并列举其他偏旁相同的字** Circle the radicals of the following characters and list some other characters sharing the same radicals

你：_____

她：_____

☐ **4. 把词语与相应的拼音连起来** Match the words with *pinyin*

bàba　dìdi　māma　gēge　jiějie　mèimei　nǎinai　yéye

爷爷　奶奶　爸爸　妈妈　哥哥　姐姐　弟弟　妹妹

☐ **5. 写汉字** Write down the characters according to the radicals and *pinyin*

（1）老师_____好。 亻（hěn）

（2）你累_____？ 口（ma）

（3）我不_____。 忄（máng）

（4）她是我_____ _____。 女（māma）

（5）谢谢_____ _____。 可（gēge）

第 3 课

一、词组：认读 Read the phrases

学习英语　　　学习法语　　　学习日语　　　学习韩国语

你姓什么　　　她姓什么

老师叫什么名字　　　你爸爸叫什么名字

二、句子：认读并连线 Read and match

1. 您贵姓？　　　A. 他姓王。

2. 他姓什么？　　　B. 我学习英语。

3. 你学习什么？　　　C. 他学习汉语。

4. 你哥哥学习什么？　　　D. 我姓白，我叫白丽娜。

三、对话 & 短文：认读并完成练习 Read the dialogue or passage and do the exercises

（一）

A：老师，您贵姓？

B：我姓李。

A：李老师好！

B：你好！你叫什么名字？

A：我叫王娜。

B：你学习什么？

A：我学习英语和日语。

☐ 读后填空 Fill in the blanks with proper words

1. 老师姓_____，学生姓_____。

2. 王娜学习_____和英语。

（二）

你们好！我姓韩，叫韩小兰。我学习法语。法语老师叫安娜。她很忙。

我弟弟学习日语，我妹妹学习韩国语。我们学习很忙。

☐ 读后判断对错 True or false (√ / ×)

（1）"我"的名字叫韩小兰。　　　　　　（　）

（2）"我"学习韩国语。　　　　　　　　（　）

（3）安娜学习法语。　　　　　　　　　（　）

（4）我弟弟妹妹不学习法语。　　　　　（　）

（5）我很忙，我弟弟妹妹不忙。　　　　（　）

四、汉字 Characters

（一）学一学 Let's learn

叫¹　什¹　么¹　名¹　字¹　贵¹　姓²　习¹　汉¹　语¹　英²　法²
日¹　韩⁷　国¹

1. 汉字的派生笔画② Derived strokes of Chinese characters ②

笔画 Stroke	名称 Name	例字 Example
㇀	hénggōu 横钩	你
亅	shùgōu 竖钩	你
㇂	xiégōu 斜钩	我
㇁	wāngōu 弯钩	（family） 家
㇃	wògōu 卧钩	（heart） 心
㇈	shùwāngōu 竖弯钩	老

2. 汉字的基本结构② Basic structures of Chinese characters ②

包围结构 Enclosed structure		例字 Example	图解 Illustration
quánbāowéi jiégòu 全包围结构 Full enclosed structure		国	
bànbāowéi jiégòu 半包围结构 Partly enclosed structure	sān miàn bāowéi 三 面 包围 Enclosed on 3 sides	（net） 网 （medicine） 医	
	liǎng miàn bāowéi 两 面 包围 Enclosed on 2 sides	（shop） 店 这	

3. 汉字的基本笔顺② Basic stroke order of Chinese characters ②

规则 Rule	例字 Example	笔顺 Stroke order
xiān zhōngjiān hòu liǎng biān 先 中间 后 两边	小	亅 小 小
cóng wài dào nèi 从 外 到 内	间	门 间
xiān lǐtou hòu fēng kǒu 先 里头 后 封 口	国	冂 国 国

4. 偏旁② Radicals ②

偏旁 Radical	名称 Name	例字 Example	说明 Explanation
口	kǒuzìpáng 口字旁	叫、吃	kǒu（mouth） 口
讠	yánzìpáng 言字旁	语、词	yán（speech） 言

（二）练一练 Let's practice

1. 加部件，变新字 Add a radical to make a new character

例：你 → 您　（1）生 → ☐　（2）十 → ☐

2. 把词语与相应的拼音连起来 Match the words with pinyin

shénme　Fǎyǔ　guìxìng　míngzi　Hánguó

法语　名字　贵姓　韩国　什么

3. 圈出下列汉字的偏旁并列举其他偏旁相同的字 Circle the radicals of the following characters and list some other characters sharing the same radicals

谢：

吃：_____

☐ 4. 写汉字 **Write down the characters according to the radicals and** *pinyin*

（1）请问您_____姓。 贝（guì）

（2）她_____李娜。 口（jiào）

（3）哥哥学英_____。 讠（yǔ）

（4）你妈妈姓_____么？ 亻（shén）

（5）我学_____不累。 乛（xí）

第 4 课

一、词组：认读 Read the phrases

汉语词典　　　英语词典　　　英汉词典　　　汉日词典

中国朋友的书包　韩国学生的书包　留学生的书包

好吃的饺子　　　好吃的面条　　　好吃的蛋炒饭

他也是留学生　　姐姐也吃饺子　　面条也很好吃

二、句子：认读并连线 Read and match

1. 这是什么词典？　　　A. 他是我哥哥。

2. 你是留学生吗？　　　B. 这是我朋友的笔。

3. 他是谁？　　　　　　C. 这是《英汉词典》。

4. 这是谁的笔？　　　　D. 不是，我是中国学生。

三、对话 & 短文：认读并完成练习 Read the dialogue or passage and do the exercises

（一）

A：这是什么？

B：这是饺子，也叫水饺。

A：饺子是包子吗？

B：饺子是饺子，不是包子。

A：饺子好吃吗？

B：很好吃。

读后填空 Fill in the blanks with proper words

饺子也叫_____，很_____。

（二）

我叫久井真一，是日本留学生。我学习汉语。这是我的书包，我的笔、本子、汉语书、《汉日词典》。

她叫久井美子。她是我姐姐，我是她弟弟。我们是姐弟，也是好朋友。她不是学生，她是老师，她教日语。那是姐姐的《日汉词典》。

1. 猜一猜 Guess the meaning of the underlined word according to the context

教(jiāo)： A. to learn   B. to teach

2. 读后判断对错 True or false (√ / ×)

（1）久井真一是学生。　　　　　　　　　（　）

（2）《日汉词典》是姐姐的。　　　　　　（　）

（3）美子、真一是姐妹。　　　　　　　　（　）

（4）真一是好学生，美子也是好学生。　　（　）

（5）美子学习日语。　　　　　　　　　　（　）

四、汉字 Characters

（一）学一学 Let's learn

这¹ 那¹ 是¹ 饺² 子¹ 包¹ 面¹ 条¹ 蛋¹ 炒⁶ 饭¹ 吃¹
谁¹ 的¹ 书¹ 本¹ 笔² 词² 典² 矿⁴ 泉⁴ 水¹ 朋¹ 友¹
也¹ 留²

☐ 1. 汉字的派生笔画③ Derived strokes of Chinese characters ③

笔画 Stroke	名称 Name	例字 Example
乛	héngzhégōu 横折钩	习
乚	héngzhétí 横折提	语
㇈	héngzhéxiégōu 横折斜钩	气
㇈	héngzhéwāngōu 横折弯钩	九
㇈	héngzhéwān 横折弯	没
㇈	héngzhézhé 横折折	（concave） 凹

☐ 2. 偏旁③ Radicals ③

偏旁 Radical	名称 Name	例字 Example	说明 Explanation
饣	shízìpáng 食字旁	饭、饺	shí（food） 食
𥫗	zhúzìtóu 竹字头	笔	zhú（bamboo） 竹

（二）练一练 Let's practice

☐ **1. 加部件，变新字** Add a radical to make a new character

例：你 → 您

（1）水 → ☐　　（2）也 → ☐☐　　（3）子 → ☐☐

☐ **2. 把词语与相应的拼音连起来** Match the words with *pinyin*

miàntiáo　cídiǎn　péngyou　Rìběn　shūbāo

日本　面条　书包　词典　朋友

☐ **3. 圈出下列汉字的偏旁并列举其他偏旁相同的字** Circle the radicals of the following characters and list some other characters sharing the same radicals

饺：_____

吗：_____

☐ **4. 写汉字** Write down the characters according to the radicals and *pinyin*

（1）蛋炒_____很好吃。　饣（fàn）

（2）这是谁的_____？　　竹（bǐ）

（3）他是_____国人。　　氵（fǎ）

（4）这是_____语词典。　氵（hàn）

（5）她是我朋_____。　　𠂇（you）

五、看图写句子　Complete the sentences according to the pictures

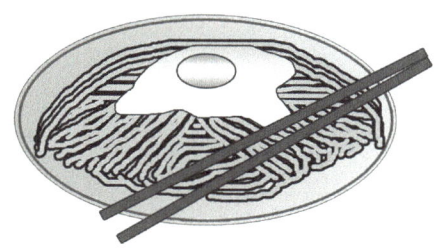

1. _____ 。

2. 他们 _____ 。

第 5 课

一、词组：认读 Read the phrases

美国学生　　英国老师　　法国朋友　　日本留学生

认识他　　　认识你　　　认识老师　　认识朋友

去商店　　　去食堂　　　去饭馆　　　去图书馆

回宿舍　　　回国　　　　现在很忙　　现在很累

现在很好　　现在不高兴　最近不忙　　最近不累

最近还可以　　　　　　　最近马马虎虎

二、句子：认读并连线 Read and match

1. 你是中国人吗？　　　A. 认识，她是我朋友的女朋友。
2. 他们去哪儿？　　　　B. 不是，我是日本人。
3. 你认识她吗？　　　　C. 是啊！
4. 好久不见了！　　　　D. 我不回宿舍，我去图书馆。
5. 最近怎么样？　　　　E. 最近我很累。
6. 你现在回宿舍吗？　　F. 他们去食堂。

三、对话 & 短文：认读并完成练习 Read the dialogue or passage and do the exercises

（一）

A：娜娜，好久不见！

B：是啊，丽丽。你最近怎么样？忙吗？

A：还可以。我现在学习汉语，很忙。你呢？

B：我很好。这是我的男(nán)朋友，丁强。丁强，这是我的好朋友，丽丽。

A：你好，丁强，认识你很高兴。

C：你好，丽丽，认识你我也很高兴。

想一想：A、B、C叫什么名字？What's the name of A, B and C?

❑ **1. 猜一猜 Guess the meaning of the underlined word according to the context**

男(nán)： A. male   B. female

❑ **2. 读后填空 Fill in the blanks with proper words**

丽丽是娜娜的_____朋友。她现在学习_____，所以(suǒyǐ so)最近很_____。丁强是娜娜的_____朋友，认识娜娜的朋友，他很_____。

（二）

王兰是中国人，她学习英语。她的语法很好，但是口语不好。她的朋友叫马小美，是美国人。马小美的爸爸是中国人，姓马，妈妈是美国人。她的汉语口语很好，但是汉字不好。王兰教小美学习汉字，小美教王兰英语口语。现在她们去图书馆借(jiè)书，王兰借英语书，小美借汉英词典。

想一想：课文里说了几个人？他们是谁？How many persons are mentioned in the text? Who are they?

1. 读后判断对错 True or false (√/×)

（1）王兰的英语口语很好。　　　　　　　　　　（　）

（2）马小美的妈妈是中国人。　　　　　　　　　（　）

（3）小美的汉字不好。　　　　　　　　　　　　（　）

（4）小美教王兰英语，王兰教小美汉语。　　　　（　）

（5）现在王兰和小美去借书。　　　　　　　　　（　）

2. 猜一猜 Guess and match the underlined words with *pinyin* and the meaning

jiè	语法	Chinese character
kǒuyǔ	口语	to borrow
yǔfǎ	汉字	oral language
Hànzì	借	grammar

四、汉字 Characters

（一）学一学 Let's learn

哪¹	人¹	认¹	识¹	高¹	兴¹	现¹	在¹	去¹	儿¹	商¹	店¹
食²	堂²	馆¹	图¹	呢¹	回¹	宿⁵	舍⁵	久²	了¹	啊²	最¹
近²	怎¹	样¹	还¹	可²	以²	马¹	虎⁵				

1. 汉字的派生笔画④ Derived strokes of Chinese characters ④

笔画 Stroke	名称 Name	例字 Example
㇉	shùzhézhégōu 竖折折钩	马

乛	héngpiěwāngōu 横撇弯钩	那
了	héngzhézhépiě 横折折撇	（extreme） 极
3	héngzhézhézhégōu 横折折折钩	奶
弓	héngzhézhézhé 横折折折	（convex） 凸
ㄣ	shùzhépiě 竖折撇	（concentrate） 专
ㄅ	shùzhézhé 竖折折	（ding, ancient tripod） 鼎

2. 汉字的造字方法① Formation of Chinese characters ①

xiàngxíngzì
象形字：用线条画出事物大概的样子。Pictograph Characters: outlining the rough shape of things with simple lines.

3. 偏旁④ Radicals ④

偏旁 Radical	名称 Name	例字 Example	说明 Explanation
辶	zǒuzhīpáng 走之旁	近、这	to walk; road
宀	bǎogàitóu 宝盖头	宿、字	roof

口	国字框 (guózìkuàng)	国、图	border
人	人字头 (rénzìtóu)	食、舍	人 (person)

（二）练一练 Let's practice

☐ **1. 加部件，变新字 Add a radical to make a new character**

例：你 → 您

（1）见 → ☐　　（2）乍 → ☐　　（3）那 → ☐

（4）不 → ☐　　（5）去 → ☐　　（6）人 → ☐

（7）尼 → ☐　　（8）马 → ☐ ☐

☐ **2. 把词语与相应的拼音连起来 Match the words with pinyin**

sùshè　　shítáng　　fànguǎn　　shāngdiàn　　zuìjìn

食堂　　商店　　宿舍　　最近　　饭馆

☐ **3. 列举跟下列汉字偏旁相同的字 List some other characters sharing the same radicals with the characters given**

国：_____

这：_____

语：_____

☐ **4. 写汉字 Write down the characters according to the radicals and pinyin**

（1）马义，好久不见了。最_____忙吗？辶（jìn）

（2）饭_____的包子还可以。饣（guǎn）

（3）现在我回宿舍，你_____？口（ne）

（4）我很累，现在我去_____堂。入（shí）

（5）我_____识他哥哥。讠（rèn）

（6）你去商_____吗？广（diàn）

（7）妈妈很_____兴。亠（gāo）

（8）你爸妈怎么_____？木（yàng）

五、看图写句子 Construct sentences according to the pictures with the words given

1. 认识

_____。

2. 去

_____。

第 6 课

一、认读词组 Read the phrases

我的一天　　　　七点起床　　　　七点半吃饭　　　　八点半上课

中午差十分十二点下课　　　　晚上差一刻十二点睡觉

去食堂　　　　去商店　　　　到图书馆　　　　到机场

每天学习太忙了　　　　学习汉语不太累

二、认读句子并连线 Read and match

1. 现在几点？　　　　　　　　A. 是啊，每天都学。

2. 我们去图书馆吧。　　　　　B. 好啊。

3. 你晚上几点睡觉？　　　　　C. 我们**都不是**中国学生。

4. 你每天都学习汉语吗？　　　D. **不都是**，我是留学生，他不是。

5. 你们都是中国学生吗？　　　E. 现在差十分十二点。

6. 你们都是留学生吗？　　　　F. 我晚上十一点半睡觉。

三、对话 & 短文：认读并完成练习 Read the dialogue or passage and do the exercises

（一）

A：真一，你们早上几点上课？

B：我们八点半上课。

A：现在八点一刻，起床吧。

B：真的吗，妈妈？

A：真的！你每天都<u>迟到</u>（chídào），老师很不高兴。

B：好，我现在起床，<u>马上</u>（mǎshàng）去上课。

A：你吃早饭吗？

B：我不吃早饭。中午见。

想一想：A、B 是谁？ Who is A, who is B?

☐ **1. 读后判断对错** True or false (√/×)

（1）现在八点十五。　　　　　　　　　（　）

（2）真一每天 8:30 上课。　　　　　　　（　）

（3）真一每天都不迟到。　　　　　　　（　）

（4）真一不吃早饭。　　　　　　　　　（　）

☐ **2. 猜一猜** Guess the meaning of the underlined words according to the context

（1）迟到（chídào）： A. to be late　　B. to be on time

（2）马上（mǎshàng）： A. later on　　B. right now

（二）

我叫中川美子，这是我弟弟，他叫中川太一。我们都是留学生，我们都学习汉语。我们上午上课，下午也上课。每天都很忙，也很累。

爸爸、妈妈的飞机下午三点到北京，我们 1:45 <u>出发</u>（chūfā）去机场。

找一找短文中的名字，说一说，你是怎么找到的？ Can you find out the names in the text? How did you find them?

1. 猜一猜 Guess the meaning of the underlined word according to the context

出_{chūfā}发：A. to arrive at　B. to set off, to set out

2. 读后填空 Fill in the blanks with proper words

中川美子的_____叫中川太一。他们都是_____，都学习_____。他们上午、下午_____上课，学习很忙也很_____。他们的爸爸妈妈下午到_____，他们差一刻两点去_____。

四、汉字 Characters

（一）学一学 Let's learn

分¹ 几¹ 点¹ 床¹ 吧¹ 飞¹ 机¹ 到¹ 场¹ 半¹ 下¹ 课¹
晚¹ 睡¹ 觉¹ 每³ 天¹ 上¹ 早¹ 中¹ 午¹ 真¹ 太¹ 刻²
都² 零¹ 差¹

1. 汉字的造字方法② Formation of Chinese characters ②

指_{zhǐshìzì}事字：用笔画表示象征意义或在象形字上加一笔表示抽象的意义。

Indicative characters: expressing symbolic meaning with strokes or adding a stroke carrying abstract meaning to a pictogram.

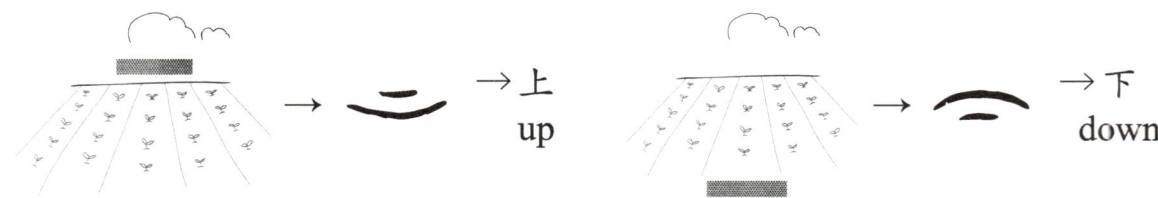

第6课

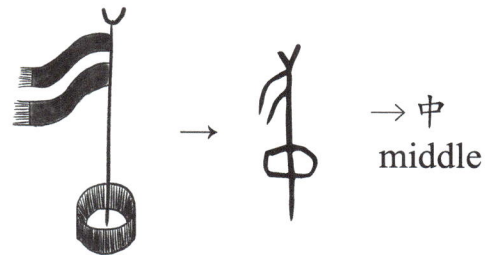 → 中 middle

☐ **2. 偏旁⑤ Radicals ⑤**

偏旁 Radical	名称 Name	例字 Example	说明 Explanation
广	guǎngzìpáng 广字旁	店、床	guǎng（wide） 广
刂	lìdāopáng 立刀旁	刻、到	dāo（knife） 刀
目	mùzìpáng 目字旁	睡	mù（eye） 目
日/日	rìzìpáng/tóu 日字旁/头	晚、早	（Sun, day） 日

（二）练一练 Let's practice

☐ **1. 把词语与相应的拼音连起来 Match the words with *pinyin***

qǐchuáng   shuìjiào   fēijī   jīchǎng   měi tiān

机场   起床   每天   飞机   睡觉

☐ **2. 加拼音并组词 Write down *pinyin* of each character and make a word with it**

例：人（rén）<u>中国人</u>   认（rèn）<u>认识</u>

（1）几（　）_____   机（　）_____

（2）见（　）_____   觉（　）_____

3. 字谜游戏 Word puzzles

① ☐☐ / 机   ② ☐☐ 起   ③ ☐ / 书 / ☐   ④ ☐ 上 / ☐ 饭

4. 选字填空 Choose the correct characters to complete the sentences

（1）我_____点去图书馆。　　　（A. 九　B. 几）

（2）妹妹下_____不上课。　　　（A. 牛　B. 午）

（3）好久不_____了！　　　　　（A. 贝　B. 见）

（4）爸妈的_____机十点到。　　（A. 飞　B. 气）

（5）我每_____都很忙。　　　　（A. 夫　B. 天）

5. 写汉字 Write down the characters according to the radicals and pinyin

（1）现在九_____。　灬（diǎn）

（2）我们一起回宿舍_____。　口（ba）

（3）他们_____是留学生。　阝（dōu）

（4）哥哥六点三_____起床。　刂（kè）

（5）我早上七点半_____食堂。　刂（dào）

（6）老师_____天都很忙。　宀（měi）

（7）我朋友_____上十点回宿舍。　日（wǎn）

（8）你女朋友明天到北京？_____的吗？　八（zhēn）

五、看图写句子 Complete the sentences according to the pictures

1. 我早上_____。

2. 我晚上_____。

3. A：你几点<u>洗澡</u>（xǐ zǎo）？

   B：_____。

4. A：你爸爸几点<u>上班</u>（shàngbān）？几点<u>下班</u>（xiàbān）？

   B：_____。

□ 猜一猜 Guess the meaning of the underlined words according to the context

（1）洗澡　　xǐzǎo　　　v.(v-o)　　_____

（2）上班　　shàngbān　　v.　　　　_____

（3）下班　　xiàbān　　　v.　　　　_____

第 7 课

一、认读词组　Read the phrases

朋友的生日　　老师的生日　　学生的秘密　　弟弟的秘密

做作业　　　　写作业　　　　学习生词　　　学习课文

预习生词　　　预习课文　　　复习生词　　　复习课文

在教室学习汉语　在图书馆做作业　在食堂吃面条

在宿舍聊天儿　　在宿舍看电视　　在宿舍上网

二、认读句子并连线　Read and match

1. 明天星期几？　　　　　　　A. 他们星期六回国。

2. 哪天去长城？　　　　　　　B. 我的生日是六月一号。

3. 你晚上做什么？　　　　　　C. 明天星期四。

4. 你爸妈什么时候回国？　　　D. 我晚上复习、预习。

5. 您的生日是几月几号？　　　E. 星期五去长城。

三、对话 & 短文：认读并完成练习　Read the dialogue or passage and do the exercises

（一）

A：兰兰，明天是丁丁的生日，我们一起吃饭吧。

B：是吗？明天星期几？

A：明天星期五。

B：明天我爸妈到中国，我去机场。

A：你什么时候去机场？

B：下午一点半。

A：十二点半我们在教室吃蛋糕(dàngāo)，怎么样？

B：太好了！我们和丁丁一起吃蛋糕！

> 找一找对话中的时间名词。说一说，这些时间会有什么事儿发生？Find out the nouns for time in the dialogue. What will happen at that time?

1. 读后判断对错 True or false (√ / ×)

（1）今天是星期四。（ ）

（2）星期五是兰兰的生日。（ ）

（3）丁丁的爸妈明天到北京。（ ）

（4）兰兰明天中午也吃蛋糕。（ ）

2. 猜一猜 Guess the meaning of the underlined word according to the context

蛋糕(dàngāo)： A. cake　B. egg

（二）

前天是九月二十八号，周(zhōu)四，我上课，学习汉语。昨天是＿＿月＿＿号，周五，我去机场，我的爸爸妈妈到中国。今天是＿＿月＿＿号，周六。今天是妈妈的生日，我们一起吃面条。明天是＿＿月＿＿号，周日，我们去长城。后天是＿＿月＿＿号，周一，爸爸、妈妈回韩国。

这几天，我们一起聊天儿、吃饭，我很高兴。

> 填一填：昨天、今天、明天、后天是几月几号？Fill in the blanks with dates of 昨天，今天，明天 and 后天.

1. 阅读理解 Reading comprehension

（1）我是哪国人？

  A. 印尼人 B. 美国人 C. 中国人 D. 韩国人

（2）我学习什么？

  A. 日语 B. 汉语 C. 英语 D. 法语

（3）星期六是谁的生日？

  A. 我 B. 爸爸 C. 妈妈 D. 哥哥

（4）我和爸妈一起_____。

  A. 去长城 B. 看电视 C. 写作业 D. 上网

2. 猜一猜 Guess the meaning of the underlined words according to the context

（1）周（zhōu）： A. 星期 B. 年

（2）几： A. many B. a few

四、汉字 Characters

（一）学一学 Let's learn

今¹ 星¹ 期¹ 时¹ 候¹ 前¹ 昨¹ 明¹ 后¹ 月¹ 号¹ 秘⁴
密⁴ 做¹ 看¹ 电¹ 视¹ 聊⁴ 网¹ 作¹ 业² 写¹ 复² 预³
文¹ 年¹ 教¹ 室²

1. 汉字的造字方法③ Formation of Chinese characters ③

会意字（huìyìzì）：两个或多个象形字组合在一起，表示新的意义。Associative

characters: putting two or more pictographic characters together to indicate new meanings.

亻+木→休
（人）
xiū
rest

日+月→明
bright

⺮+毛→笔
（竹）
bamboo+hair
→ pen

氵+目→泪
（水）
lèi
water+eyes
→ tears

2. 偏旁⑥ Radicals ⑥

偏旁 Radical	名称 Name	例字 Example	说明 Explanation
耳	ěrzìpáng 耳字旁	聊	ěr（ear） 耳
月	yuèzìpáng 月字旁	期、明	（moon, time） 月 （on the right）
攵	fǎnwénpáng 反文旁	教	indicating an action with a stick in hand

（二）练一练 Let's practice

1. 把词语与相应的拼音连起来 Match the words with *pinyin*

yùxí   liáotiānr   kèwén   mìmì   qiánnián

秘密   聊天儿   预习   前年   课文

2. 找出相同的部件写在方格里 Find out the same component in each group and write it in the box

（1） ☐ 星 姓　　　（2） ☐ 时 对

（3） ☐ 秘 密　　　（4） ☐ 视 现

（5） ☐ 室 到　　　（6） ☐ 昨 作 怎

3. 字谜游戏 Word puzzles

① ☐／词　　② ☐ 起　　③ ☐☐／天　　④ ☐ 生／本

4. 选字填空 Choose the correct characters to complete the sentences

（1）_____天是他女朋友的生日。（A.今　B.令）

（2）这是_____天的_____业。（A.作　B.昨　C.怎）

（3）我晚上看电_____。（A.视　B.现）

（4）我每天都_____习汉_____。（A.学　B.字）

（5）_____天我不_____宿舍复习。（A.在　B.后）

5. 写汉字 Write down the characters according to the radicals and *pinyin*

（1）我的朋友在宿舍_____书。目（kàn）

（2）我们去图书馆_____作业吧。宀（xiě）

（3）我一点去教_____。宀（shì）

（4）弟弟在宿舍看电_____。礻（shì）

（5）我每天晚上都_____作业。亻（zuò）

（6）我每天都_____习生词。页（yù）

（7）你什么时_____去图书馆？亻（hou）

（8）我们星_____五去长城？月（qī）

五、看图写句子 Construct sentences according to the pictures with the words given

1. 复习

_____。

2. 星期天

_____。

第 8 课

一、认读词组 Read the phrases

大学生　　　　中学生　　　　小学生

大学老师　　　中学老师　　　小学老师

公司经理　　　公司职员　　　医院的医生　　　医院的护士(hùshi)

在公司工作　　在学校工作　　在宾馆工作　　　在医院工作

兄(xiōng)弟姐妹＝哥哥、弟弟、姐姐、妹妹

二、认读句子并连线 Read and match

1. 你家有几口人？　　　　A. 她今年二十四岁。

2. 你家都有什么人？　　　B. 我今年七十八岁。

3. 您多大年纪？　　　　　C. 我家有四口人。

4. 真一的姐姐今年多大？　D. 她九岁。

5. 玛丽的妹妹几岁？　　　E. 有爷爷、奶奶、爸爸、妈妈和我。

三、短文：认读并完成练习 Read the passages and do the exercises

（一）

我爸爸以前是大学教授(jiàoshòu professor)，现在是一个中学的校长(xiàozhǎng principal)。妈妈在医院工

> 读一读，找一找：我家有几口人？都有谁？How many people are there in my family? Who are they?

作，她不是大夫(dàifu, doctor)，她是护士(hùshi, nurse)。我大哥是个老板(lǎobǎn, boss)，有一个小公司。二哥是记者(jìzhě, journalist)，在北京电视台(diànshìtái, TV station)工作。我还有一个姐姐，是一个作家(zuòjiā, writer)。

☐ **1. 连线：他们做什么工作？** Write down the jobs in Chinese and draw lines to make matches

爸爸　妈妈　大哥　二哥　姐姐

_____　_____　_____　_____　教授 / 校长

    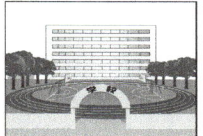

☐ **2. 加拼音并组词** Write down *pinyin* of the character and make a word with it

（1）长（cháng）_____（zhǎng）_____

（2）大（　　）_____（　　）_____

Tips: There are many "多音字 (duōyīnzì, polyphonic characters)" in Chinese. Different pronounciations of the polyphonic characters indicate different meanings. Another example, 教 jiāo is a verb, which means to teach something, while 教 jiào is a noun and used in words like 教室 or 教授.

（二）

我叫丁娜娜，今年32岁，是一个导游(dǎoyóu, tour guide)。我每年都去很多(duō, many)国家，认识很多外国朋友。我的法国朋友是外交官(wàijiāoguān, diplomat)，在大使馆工作。我的美国朋友是一个警察(jǐngchá, policeman)。我还有一个韩国朋友，他现在在三星公司工作。

☐ 1. 猜一猜 Guess the meaning of the underlined words according to the context

（1）国家： A. country B. home

（2）外国： A. motherland B. foreign country

（3）大使馆： A. embassy B. government

你用什么办法猜到这些词的意思的？What strategy did you use to guess the meaning of the words?

☐ 2. 回答问题 Answer the questions

（1）丁娜娜今年多大？

（2）丁娜娜做什么工作？

（3）丁娜娜<u>wèi shénme（why）</u>认识很多外国朋友？

☐ 3. 连线 Draw lines to make matches

公司职员

wàijiāoguān
外交官

jǐngchá
警察

四、汉字 Characters

（一）学一学 Let's learn

家¹ 有¹ 口¹ 没¹ 多¹ 大¹ 纪³ 岁¹ 工¹ 公² 司² 经²
理² 医¹ 律⁴ 职³ 员³ 和¹ 售⁴ 货⁴ 校¹ 院¹ 宾⁵

1. 汉字的造字方法④ Formation of Chinese characters ④

xíngshēngzì
形声字：由提示意义和提示发音的部件组成。Phonograms: combining a meaning radical and a sound radical.

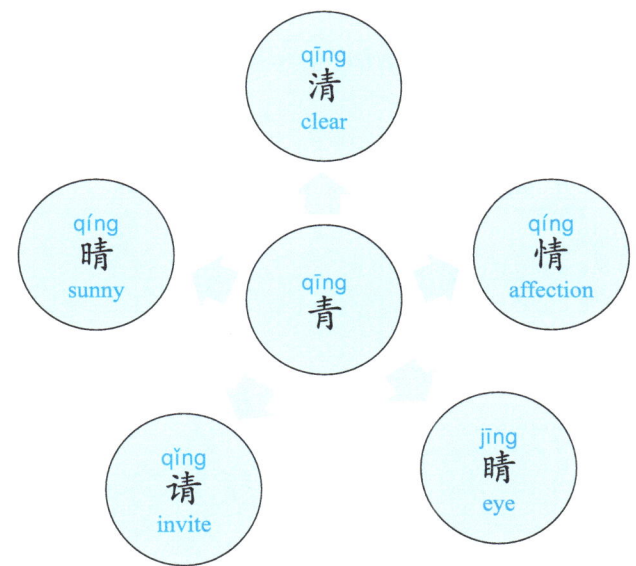

2. 偏旁⑦ Radicals ⑦

偏旁 Radical	名称 Name	例字 Example	说明 Explanation
氵	sāndiǎnshuǐ 三点水	没、汉	（water） 水
贝/贝	bèizìpáng/dǐ 贝字旁/底	cái（wealth） 财、货	bèi（seashell; money） 贝

第8课

41

阝	ěrdāopáng 耳刀旁	院	hill; terrain (on the left)
彳	shuānglìrén 双立人	很、律	street

（二）练一练 Let's practice

☐ **1. 把词语与相应的拼音连起来** Match the words with *pinyin*

bīnguǎn　　jīnglǐ　　zhíyuán　　lǜshī　　niánjì

经理　律师　职员　年纪　宾馆

☐ **2. 加拼音并组词** Write down *pinyin* of each character and make a word with it

例：人（ rén ）中国人　　　　认（ rèn ）认识

（1）马（　　）＿＿＿＿＿　　玛（　　）＿＿＿＿＿

　　妈（　　）＿＿＿＿＿　　吗（　　）＿＿＿＿＿

（2）司（　　）＿＿＿＿＿　　词（　　）＿＿＿＿＿

（3）作（　　）＿＿＿＿＿　　昨（　　）＿＿＿＿＿

（4）姓（　　）＿＿＿＿＿　　星（　　）＿＿＿＿＿

（5）店（　　）＿＿＿＿＿　　点（　　）＿＿＿＿＿

（6）官（　　）＿＿＿＿＿　　馆（　　）＿＿＿＿＿

（7）饺（　　）＿＿＿＿＿　　校（　　）＿＿＿＿＿

3. 字谜游戏 Word puzzles

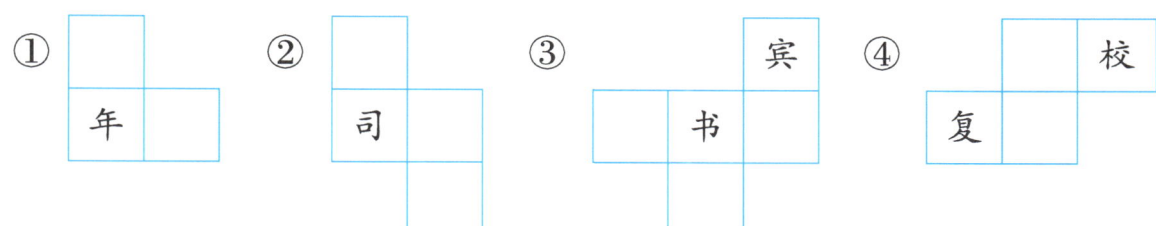

4. 选字填空 Choose the correct characters to complete the sentences

（1）我哥哥不是_____机。　　　　　（A. 司　B. 同）

（2）你爸妈今年多大年_____？　　　（A. 记　B. 纪）

（3）请问，您_____姓？　　　　　　（A. 员　B. 贵）

（4）我八点零五_____去_____司。　（A. 公　B. 分）

5. 写汉字 Write down the characters according to the radicals and *pinyin*

（1）我_____有四口人。　宀（jiā）

（2）小朋友，你今年几_____？　山（suì）

（3）她哥哥是三星公司的职_____。　贝（yuán）

（4）我们学_____有很多留学生。　木（xiào）

（5）我姐姐是_____生。　匚（yī）

（6）你奶奶多大年_____？　纟（jì）

（7）我哥哥是公司经_____？　王（lǐ）

（8）他爸妈都在医_____工作。　阝（yuàn）

五、看图写句子 Complete the sentences according to the pictures

1. 他是_____。

2. 我在_____。

3. 她爸爸是_____。

4. 你姐姐是_____吗?

第 9 课

一、认读词组　Read the phrases

一个面包	两个苹果	三个草莓	四斤苹果	五斤香蕉
六支笔	七瓶啤酒	八杯咖啡	九瓶矿泉水	十本英语书
怎么卖	怎么写	买水果	买面包	买书包　买本子
一毛钱	两块钱	五十块钱	一百(bǎi)块钱	没有零钱
真贵	真酸	真忙	真累	
贵死了	酸死了	忙死了	累死了	

二、认读句子并连线　Read and match

1. 苹果怎么卖？　　　　　　A. 酸死了！
2. 你有零钱吗？　　　　　　B. 我不买。
3. 一共多少钱？　　　　　　C. 我买一杯。
4. 橘子甜吗？　　　　　　　D. 六块五一斤。
5. 你买几杯咖啡？　　　　　E. 我没有零钱。
6. 你买啤酒吗？　　　　　　F. 二十七块钱。

三、短文：认读并完成练习　Read the passages and do the exercises

（一）

学校有一家食品(shípǐn)店，这家店有很多吃的东西。王小娜每个星期都去那儿买东西。这个星期，她买饼<ruby>干<rt>bǐnggān</rt></ruby>、牛奶和葡<ruby>萄<rt>pútao</rt></ruby>。饼干有两 <ruby>种<rt>zhǒng</rt></ruby>：一种是牛奶饼干，五块钱一<ruby>袋<rt>dài</rt></ruby>；一种是<ruby>巧克力<rt>qiǎokèlì</rt></ruby>饼干，六块钱一袋。牛奶也有两种：小的每<ruby>盒<rt>hé</rt></ruby>半斤，四块钱；大的每盒一<ruby>公斤<rt>gōngjīn</rt></ruby>，十二块钱。葡萄也有大的和小的两种：大的十块钱一斤，小的八块。她买一袋巧克力饼干，两小盒牛奶，还有一斤半大葡萄。

短文中画线的生词，哪些是名词，哪些是量词？你是怎么猜的？ Which underlined words are nouns and which ones are measure words? What strategy did you apply?

1. 猜一猜 Guess the meaning of the underlined words according to the context

Nouns	① _____	chocolate
	② _____	grapes
	③ _____	cookies, biscuit
	④ _____	food
Measure words	⑤ _____	kilo
	⑥ _____	kind
	⑦ _____	box
	⑧ _____	bag

2. 填表 Fill in the form according to the passage

牛奶（250g）：_____元/盒	牛奶（1000g）：_____元/盒
牛奶饼干：_____元/袋	巧克力饼干：_____元/袋
大葡萄：_____元/斤	小葡萄：_____元/斤

3. 回答问题 Answer the questions

（1）这个星期王小娜都买什么？

（2）王小娜一共花(huā to spend)多少钱？

（二）

今天，我的朋友和我一起去买东西。我买一支牙膏(yā gāo)、一把伞(bǎ sǎn)。我的朋友买一个笔记本(bǐjìběn)、一支笔。我一共花(huā to spend)九十九块钱。我给(gěi to give)售货员100块钱，她找(zhǎo to give change)我一块钱。我朋友一共花十二块，他没有零钱，也给售货员100块钱。

1. 阅读理解 Reading comprehension

（1）我朋友买什么？

    A. 牙膏   B. 本子   C. 伞   D. 水

（2）售货员找(zhǎo to give change)我朋友多少钱？

    A. 1块钱   B. 12块钱   C. 88块钱   D. 99块钱

2. 写一写以下物品的名称 Write down the names of the following items

跟同学们分享一下，你用了什么方法找到了这些词？Share with your classmates how you found the words for the pictures.

四、汉字 Characters

（一）学一学 Let's learn

苹³ 果¹ 卖² 买¹ 小¹ 少¹ 钱¹ 瓶¹ 块¹ 元¹ 个¹ 啤³
酒² 咖³ 啡³ 杯¹ 贩⁷ 两¹ 请¹ 问¹ 斤² 香³ 蕉³ 草²
莓* 橘⁷ 共² 毛¹ 角² 甜³ 尝⁵ 哎⁷ 呀⁴ 酸⁴ 死³

1. 偏旁⑧ Radicals ⑧

偏旁 Radical	名称 Name	例字 Example	说明 Explanation
木/朩	mùzìpáng 木字旁	zhuō（table） 机、橘、桌	mù（wood） 木
艹	cǎozìtóu 草字头	草、苹	（grass） 草
钅	jīnzìpáng 金字旁	钱	jīn（metal） 金

第 9 课

（二）练一练 Let's practice

☐ **1. 把词语与相应的拼音连起来** Match the words with *pinyin*

píjiǔ   cǎoméi   xiāngjiāo   píngguǒ   kāfēi

香蕉   咖啡   草莓   苹果   啤酒

☐ **2. 列举跟下列汉字偏旁相同的字** List some other characters sharing the same radicals with the characters given

货：＿＿＿＿＿＿＿＿＿＿＿＿＿＿＿＿

吗：＿＿＿＿＿＿＿＿＿＿＿＿＿＿＿＿

蕉：＿＿＿＿＿＿＿＿＿＿＿＿＿＿＿＿

☐ **3. 字谜游戏** Word puzzles

① 包   ② 么   ③ 水

☐ **4. 选字填空** Choose the correct characters to complete the sentences

（1）那个小贩＿＿＿水果。　　　　（A. 买　B. 卖）

（2）这支＿＿＿两块五＿＿＿钱。　（A. 毛　B. 笔）

（3）请＿＿＿，这本＿＿＿典多少钱？（A. 问　B. 词）

（4）她＿＿＿天都吃草＿＿＿。　　（A. 莓　B. 每）

☐ **5. 写汉字** Write down the characters according to the radicals and *pinyin*

（1）丽丽每天上午都买一＿＿＿咖啡。　木（bēi）

49

（2）我哥哥去买啤_____。氵（jiǔ）

（3）三斤苹果一共十五_____。土（kuài）

（4）我没有零_____。钅（qián）

（5）_____问，这儿有橘子吗？讠（qǐng）

（6）苹果怎么_____？十（mài）

（7）我买两个_____蕉。日（xiāng）

（8）你尝尝_____莓。艹（cǎo）

五、看图写句子 Construct sentences according to the pictures with the words given

1. 买

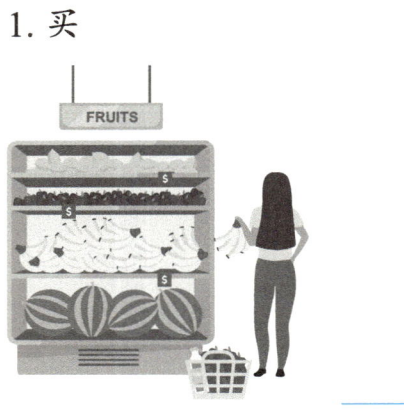

2. 甜

第 10 课

一、汉字 Characters

（一）学一学 Let's learn

周² 末² 愉⁶ 快¹ 东¹ 西¹ 位² 给¹ 介¹ 绍¹ 长² 得²
漂² 亮² 照² 女¹ 礼² 物² 来¹ 爱¹

偏旁⑨ Radicals ⑨

偏旁 Radical	名称 Name	例字 Example	说明 Explanation
礻	shìzìpáng 示字旁	礼、视	shì（to pray; to bless） 示
牜	niúzìpáng 牛字旁	物	niú（cow, cattle） 牛
灬	sìdiǎndǐ 四点底	照、点	huǒ（fire） 火

（二）练一练 Let's practice

1. 把词语与相应的拼音连起来 Match the words with *pinyin*

dōngxi　nǚ'ér　lǐwù　piàoliang　yúkuài

愉快　东西　礼物　漂亮　女儿

2. 选字填空 Choose the correct characters to complete the sentences

（1）周_____你去哪儿？　　　　　　（A. 未　B. 末）

（2）一共三十_____钱。　　　　　　（A. 块　B. 快）

（3）我给他_____绍一_____女朋友。（A. 个　B. 介）

（4）她姐姐长_____漂亮。　　　　　（A. 得　B. 很）

3. 写汉字 Write down the characters according to the radicals and *pinyin*

（1）老师的女儿很可_____。 ⺌（ài）

（2）我_____朋友买一本书。 纟（gěi）

（3）他的姐姐很漂_____。 宀（liang）

（4）认识你很高兴，请多多关_____。 灬（zhào）

（5）我介_____一下，这是我爷爷。 纟（shào）

（6）_____末你去哪儿？ 冂（zhōu）

（7）这_____是我的汉语老师。 亻（wèi）

（8）妹妹给我买一个礼_____。 牛（wù）

二、句子 Sentences

（一）家庭 Family
jiātíng

1. 回答问题 Answer the questions

（1）你家有几口人？

（2）你家都有谁？

第10课

❏ **2. 根据回答画一画 Draw your family tree according to the answers above**

（二）家人 **Family members**

❏ **1. 怎样介绍一个人 How to introduce a person**

	问题 Questions	回答 Answers
年纪		
工作		
学习		
（appearance）样子		

53

2. 根据实际情况，在家庭树上添加信息 Add details to the family tree

三、写作格式与标点符号 Format and punctuations

（一）作文格式 Format for composition

　　1. 标题空四个格或居中。Leave four boxes before the title or put the title in the middle.

　　2. 每段空两格，从第三个格开始写。Leave two boxes before you write each paragraph.

（二）常用标点符号① Frequently used punctuations ①

　　。句号 jùhào　　！叹号 tànhào　　？问号 wènhào

　　，逗号 dòuhào　　、顿号 dùnhào　　：冒号 màohào

1. 标点符号单独占一格。Each punctuation takes up one box.

2. 标点符号一般不能写在每行第一个格，而应该写在前一行末尾。If the last character of the sentences takes up the last box of the line, the punctuation should be put outside the box, right after the last character, rather than the first box of the next line.

四、作文 Composition

　　以《我的家庭》为题，写一篇作文，不少于60字 Write a composition entitled "my family" (no less than 60 characters)

第 10 课

第 10 课

附 录

补充词表 Supplementary New Words[*]

第2课

| 但是 [2] | dànshì | conj. | but |

第4课

| 教 [1] | jiāo | v. | to teach |

第5课

男 [1]	nán	adj.	male
语法 [4]	yǔfǎ	n.	grammar
口语 [4]	kǒuyǔ	n.	oral language
借 [2]	jiè	v.	to borrow

第6课

迟到 [4]	chídào	v.	to be late
马上 [1]	mǎshàng	adv.	right now, immediately
出发 [2]	chūfā	v.	to set off, to set out
洗澡 [2]	xǐzǎo	v.(v-o)	to have a shower/bath
上班 [1]	shàngbān	v.	to go to work
下班 [1]	xiàbān	v.	to go off work

第7课

| 蛋糕 [5] | dàngāo | n. | cake |
| 周 [2] | zhōu | n. | week |

---

[*] Students are supposed to master these words.

几 [1]	jǐ	pron.	a few

第 8 课

大使馆 [3]	dàshǐguǎn	n.	embassy
外交官 [4]	wàijiāoguān	n.	diplomat
教授 [4]	jiàoshòu	n.	professor
校长 [2]	xiàozhǎng	n.	principal
大夫 [3]	dàifu	n.	doctor
护士 [4]	hùshi	n.	nurse
老板 [3]	lǎobǎn	n.	boss
导游 [4]	dǎoyóu	n.	tour guide
记者 [3]	jìzhě	n.	journalist
作家 [2]	zuòjiā	n.	writer
警察 [3]	jǐngchá	n.	policeman
电视台 [3]	diànshìtái	n.	TV station
国家 [1]	guójiā	n.	country
外国 [1]	wàiguó	n.	foreign country

第 9 课

食品 [3]	shípǐn	n.	food
饼干 [5]	bǐnggān	n.	cookies, biscuit
葡萄 [5]	pútao	n.	grapes
巧克力 [4]	qiǎokèlì	n.	chocolate
伞 [4]	sǎn	n.	umbrella
笔记本 [2]	bǐjìběn	n.	notebook
种 [3]	zhǒng	m.	kind
袋 [4]	dài	n.	bag
盒 [5]	hé	n.	box
公斤 [2]	gōngjīn	m.	kilo

把 [3]	bǎ	m.	(for things with a handle eg. knife, umbrella, chair, key, etc.)
花 [2]	huā	v.	to spend
找 [1]	zhǎo	v.	to give change
给 [1]	gěi	v.	to give

第 10 课

| 家庭 | jiātíng | n. | family |
| 样子 | yàngzi | n. | appearance |

图书在版编目（CIP）数据

汉语十日通．读写．入门篇/程璐璐主编．—北京：商务印书馆，2023
ISBN 978-7-100-21971-6

Ⅰ.①汉…　Ⅱ.①程…　Ⅲ.①汉语—阅读教学—对外汉语教学—教材　②汉语—写作—对外汉语教学—教材　Ⅳ.① H195.4

中国国家版本馆 CIP 数据核字（2023）第 024129 号

权利保留，侵权必究。

汉语十日通
读写·入门篇
程璐璐　主编

商 务 印 书 馆 出 版
（北京王府井大街36号　邮政编码100710）
商 务 印 书 馆 发 行
北京捷迅佳彩印刷有限公司印刷
ISBN 978-7-100-21971-6

2023年5月第1版　　开本 889×1194　1/16
2023年5月北京第1次印刷　印张 4¾

定价：48.00元